NEWSPAPERS & MAGAZINES

Technology • People • Process

JULIAN PETLEY

HODDER
Wayland

an imprint of Hodder Children's Books

Mediawise series

Newspapers and Magazines   Film   Internet   Advertising

Produced for Hodder Wayland by Discovery Books Limited, Unit 3, 37 Watling Street, Leintwardine, Shropshire SY7 0LW, England

Published in Great Britain in 2002 by Hodder Wayland, an imprint of Hodder Children's Books

Editor: Patience Coster
Series editor: Victoria Brooker
Series design: Mind's Eye Design, Lewes
Artwork: Stefan Chabluk
Commissioned photographs: Chris Fairclough

With thanks to the staff of the *Western Mail* in Cardiff

British Library Cataloguing in Publication Data
Petley, Julian
Newspapers and magazines. - (Mediawise)
1. Newspapers - Juvenile literature 2. Periodicals - Juvenile literature
I. Title
302.2'32

ISBN 0 7502 4049 0

Printed and bound in Hong Kong

Hodder Children's Books, a division of Hodder Headline Limited, 338 Euston Road, London NW1 3BH

Picture acknowledgements: Bettmann/Corbis 30, 39; Corbis 4 (Steve Raymer), 8 , 32 (Peter Turnley), 9 (Mitchell Gerber), 11 (Hubert Stadler), 14 (Lynn Goldsmith), 17 (Bill Gentile), 27 (Francoise de Mulder), 29 (Michael Brennan), 36 (John Farmar; Cordaiy Photo Library Ltd), 41 (Roger Ressmeyer), 52 (Chris Bland; Eye Ubiquitous), 57 (Wally McNamee), 59 (Phil Schermeister); Mary Evans Picture Library 12, 48, 49; John Frost Historical Newspaper Service 10; Impact Photos 31, 58; Popperfoto 7, 33, 37, 40; The Stock Market 15, 47.

Cover design by Hodder Wayland
Cover photo by Kathleen Campbell, Getty Images

CONTENTS

WHAT ARE NEWSPAPERS FOR?

Newspapers are a familiar feature of daily life in all modern societies.

The obvious answer to this question is: to give people the news and to keep them informed. But open any newspaper and you will find an amazingly wide range of material covering international affairs, domestic politics, crime, pop and film stars, sport, television and radio schedules, the weather, and so on. Is all of this news? Do all newspapers carry the same mix of material? And what is the relationship between the news and the advertisements that fill so much space in our newspapers?

Features and leaders

There are some basic distinctions that can help to identify the different sorts of articles found in newspapers. For example, there are stories, which give us the latest, up-to-the-minute news, and are usually found on the front page and the immediately following ones. These stories are divided into domestic (home) news and foreign news. Then there are features, which fill in the background to current stories. And finally there are 'opinion' pieces; these are either 'leaders', anonymous articles giving a paper's particular point of view on an issue of the day, or comment columns by 'star' journalists or well-known public figures (such writers are sometimes known as 'pundits'). It is also possible to distinguish between 'hard' and 'soft' news. Hard news concerns national and international politics and current affairs. Soft news refers to 'human interest' stories: domestic dramas, gossip about television, film, and music industry personalities, UFO sightings and the like.

Locals and nationals

In terms of the newspapers themselves, we need first to distinguish between local and national ones. Some local papers are published weekly, others daily; some are distributed only in a particular town or city, others across a whole county or state. The national press is divided into Sundays and dailies, with most dailies publishing a Sunday edition.

Tabloids and broadsheets

Newspapers are published in two main sizes: broadsheet or text-size, and tabloid or half-size. The tabloid size lends itself to bolder forms of layout (the way in which the text and pictures look on the page) and cheaper full-page advertising. Tabloids are sometimes referred to as the 'popular' and broadsheets as the 'quality' or 'serious' press, but there's no necessary link between the size of a paper and the nature of its contents. For example, in France, *Libération* is a highly reputable and serious tabloid newspaper.

Media Fact

The birth of the tabloid

Tabloid was originally the brand name of a medicine first sold in the 1880s in Britain. Tabloids were tablets that were far more compact than their rivals. Most early newspapers were half-size, and therefore took on the nickname 'tabloids'. Then the broadsheet format became more popular, but from the 1960s onwards the tabloid format once again found favour. One reason for this is that tabloids are easier to read than broadsheets while travelling to or from work by public transport.

Tabloids (above) and broadsheets (below) differ in their presentation of similar news items.

So should we assume that the tabloids concentrate on 'soft' news and the broadsheets on 'hard' news? Unfortunately it is not that straightforward. Recent years have seen considerable debate about the 'tabloidization' or 'dumbing down' of the broadsheet press, which stands accused of cutting back on foreign news and coverage of domestic politics, and increasingly filling its pages with trivia and tittle-tattle. Meanwhile, it is also claimed, the tabloid press has become ever more sleazy, sensationalist and eager to intrude into people's private lives. In short, it is argued, the press as a whole has become more concerned with entertaining people than informing them, and turned into an enterprise in which commercial motives have overtaken civic ones.

Anyone interested in journalism today has to face much-discussed issues such as these. But it's useful to remember that these debates have a longer history than is often supposed.

Newspapers have always been commercial enterprises, and since the middle of the nineteenth century some of them have been very big businesses indeed. This is not to say that those who own or work for newspapers are interested solely in making money, or to deny that many of them have higher motives. It is simply to point out the fact that, as private businesses in a highly competitive market place, papers that lose money don't tend to survive, or to survive unchanged. This is particularly true in a business environment in which newspaper readership is declining, as people increasingly turn to the radio, television or internet for their news.

Today, in many countries, the internet is an increasingly important source of national and international news.

Advertising

The commercial aspect of newspaper publishing was given a tremendous boost by the enormous growth in advertising, which took place in the mid-nineteenth century. Those keen to bring their goods and services to the attention of a rapidly growing market saw advertising in newspapers as the ideal way to do so. In 1860 in the United States, the advertising content of a paper like the *Pittsburgh Gazette* was a remarkable 83 per cent. By 1879 advertising revenue accounted for $40m of American newspapers' revenue, and by 1919, 65 per cent of their total income. In Britain today, local dailies derive 60 per cent and local weeklies 80 per cent of their revenue from advertising. Meanwhile, the figure for the national tabloids is 30 per cent and for the broadsheets 70 per cent.

Media Fact

The importance of advertising

As long ago as 1886, 61 per cent of the column space of the *Daily Telegraph* and 49 per cent of *The Times* was taken up by advertising. By the 1930s nearly three-quarters of the income of the national dailies was coming from advertising revenue.

Clearly such a situation leads to intense competition. All papers desperately need to maintain their circulations, those most dependent on advertising in order to keep the advertisers happy, and those more dependent on readers in order to keep up their sales. This brings us back to the question of 'tabloidization' or 'dumbing down' because, it is often argued, in such a highly competitive environment, entertainment triumphs over information, and trivia and sensationalism drive out serious journalism.

Newspapers not only report the news; sometimes, as in the case of the collapse of President Ceaucescu's regime in Romania in 1989, they help to make it too.

The popular press – a long history

There may well be some truth in the claims made above, but it is important to bear in mind that the popular press has existed since the first half of the nineteenth century. Then, in the United Kingdom and the United States, the growing band of popular newspapers aimed at the newly literate were criticized for being as sensationalist and trivia-obsessed as today's tabloids.

So, to try to answer our opening question: what are newspapers for? Well, first of all they are there to make money for those who own them. This they do from a combination of advertising and the cover price charged to readers. Without such revenues there would simply be no newspapers at all. But they are also there to inform their readers. Heavyweight papers such as the *Financial Times* or *Washington Post* do this in a largely 'straight' fashion, with little concession to entertainment values. Others feel that their readers need entertaining as well as informing and mix the two functions. At the other end of the scale, papers such as the *Sport* or the *National Enquirer* offer little other than entertainment – of a kind. It is questions about the extent of the mix, and the nature of the entertainment on offer, which fuel so many fierce debates about the function of the press in today's society.

Star weddings – in this case that of Mariah Carey – are an ever-reliable source of 'soft' news stories and pictures.

WHAT IS A MAGAZINE?

The cover of the first British publication to describe itself as a magazine.

Walk into any newsagent and it's impossible not to be struck by the sheer number of different magazine titles on the shelves. The word 'magazine' was first used to describe something miscellaneous, a collection of different kinds of article. Many early magazines were barely distinguishable from weekly newspapers. The first person in Britain to use the word 'magazine' to describe a publication is generally thought to be the printer and publisher Edward Cave who founded the *Gentleman's Magazine* in 1731. However, publications that we would describe as magazines existed before that date, such as the *Review*, founded in 1704 by Daniel Defoe (of *Robinson Crusoe* fame), and Joseph Addison and Richard Steele's *Tatler* (1709) and *Spectator* (1711).

Significantly, the word 'magazine' derives from the French word 'magasin' meaning 'department store'. This not only indicates the all-inclusive nature of early magazines but also hints at their key commercial role. For the rise of the modern magazine, even more than that of the newspaper, is intimately bound up with the development of advertising.

In Britain the lifting of a number of taxes on the printed media, especially the tax on revenue raised by advertising, not only boosted the popular press but also gave rise to a new range of magazines such as *Pickwick* and *Penny Magazine*. These magazines were eager to appeal to a newly literate part of the population with money to spend. Meanwhile in the United States, which had yet to develop any truly national papers, magazines offered a valuable opportunity to advertise goods and services nationwide. In the 1880s E C Allen launched the *People's Literary Companion*. This magazine's main purpose was to advertise a soap powder for which Allen owned the marketing rights. The soap advertisements were scattered in between stories, fashion items and household tips, and the magazine rapidly achieved a circulation of 500,000. This mix also characterized Cyrus Curtis' *Ladies' Home Journal*, which had a readership of 750,000 by 1895. Building on a similar model, Curtis then launched the *Saturday Evening Post* which, by 1910, had a circulation of over 2,000,000.

Just a small sample of the thousands of magazines in circulation in Western societies today.

The popularity of magazines was stimulated by the development of faster typesetting and improved image-making technology, which made for a superior quality of both text and pictures. In North America in 1893, *Munsey's Journal* reduced its price to ten cents a copy: the result was a massive increase in circulation and a flood of advertisements. It was not long before *McClure's* and *Cosmopolitan* followed suit, and the era of cheap, general magazines began. By 1905 there were twenty national magazines in the USA, loaded with advertising and reaching a combined audience of 5.5 million readers. In the UK much the same thing was happening with magazines such as *Tit-Bits*, *Pearson's Weekly* and *Northcliffe's Answers* demonstrating the economic viability of cheap, well-illustrated, high-circulation journals heavily reliant on advertising revenue.

Media Fact

Women's magazines

The earliest women's magazine, *The Ladies' Mercury*, was first published in 1693 by the bookseller John Dunton. In 1770, *The Lady's Magazine* appeared, and was responsible for introducing the visual elements for which women's magazines were to become noted. Both of these early magazines were aimed at aristocratic ladies of leisure.

Target groups

Soon, however, publishers began to regard their magazines less as printed products to be sold to readers and more as vehicles which organized those readers into clearly defined target groups; these could then be sold to advertisers. Thus the audiences themselves became the 'products' generated by the media industry, and the selling of audiences to advertisers via magazines, newspapers and, later, broadcasting, became a highly sophisticated marketing strategy. Nowhere is this clearer than in the case of the magazine market, which is carefully divided ('niched') into a remarkable number and variety of different readership groups.

Then (above): working on a magazine in Brussels in 1905. And now (below): computer technology has made redundant the old methods of magazine publishing.

The most numerous magazines are consumer titles – those which provide leisure-time information and entertainment. Of these, the most common are women's titles. These can be subdivided into titles aimed at different age groups and, to some extent, at different social classes and income brackets. There is now a similarly niched, but significantly smaller, market for men's magazines too.

Specialist interest magazines

Both women's and men's magazines obviously define their audience in gender terms, but there is a vast range of magazines which do so according to their specialist interests.

One of the biggest of such groups are computer users, but others include gardeners, bird watchers, motoring fans, film buffs, do-it-yourself enthusiasts, aircraft spotters, photographers, and sportsmen and women. Such magazines derive about two-thirds of their revenue from their cover price and the rest from advertising.

Trade magazines

This is one of the fastest growing areas in journalism. These magazines, also known as business-to-business publications and 'trade mags', are aimed directly at people working within a specific area, such as medicine, the media, architecture, engineering and the like, and provide them with news of the latest developments in their industry or profession. Not only do these magazines provide a service to their specialist readerships, but they also act as a major source of news for the national press. Business and professional magazines derive about 80 per cent of their revenue from advertising.

Today's magazine market caters for an extremely wide range of special interests.

Within this sector, a recent growth area has been the controlled circulation magazine, which is distributed (usually free) to key players within specific business sectors. This form of magazine publishing first developed in the United States and was then imported into Europe. A great deal of market research goes into building up a profile of the appropriate readership and addressing them directly through both articles and advertising. Naturally, publications targeted so narrowly and at such high flyers are extremely attractive to advertisers.

In-house magazines

Finally there are the in-house magazines, of which there are two basic types. Firstly those aimed at employees of a large company, whose purpose is to keep them in touch with new developments in the company, as well as helping to develop a sense of corporate identity by keeping them in touch with one another. And secondly there are magazines aimed at the customers of big retail chains, which contain information about the products and services on offer from those stores. In-house magazines are frequently produced not by the organization itself but by a publishing company working on behalf of that organization.

The crucial role which advertising plays in the magazine sector means that those working within it are constantly faced with the difficult matter of balancing the need to attract advertising against the need to preserve editorial

The top jobs in newspaper journalism still tend to be taken by men. This is less likely to be the case in magazine publishing, especially women's magazines.

independence and the desire to keep faith with the readers. In particular, readers need to be able to feel confident that articles and news stories are not simply designed to attract and keep advertisers. They also need to be able to distinguish between, say, an *advertisement* for a new model of car in a magazine and an independent *review* of that car in the same magazine. As John Morrish puts it in his book *Magazine Editing*, 'there is no more vexed issue than the relationship between the editor and the advertising department. A certain distance is desirable if the independence and integrity of the editorial department is to be maintained'.

JOB PROFILE

The Advertising Manager

The most important task of the advertising manager of a magazine is to ensure that it attracts advertising, and does so at favourable rates. Magazines have the luxury of being able to plan their features well in advance of newspapers, and the manager will play a crucial part in this process, helping to ensure a steady flow of articles which advertisers will find attractive and with which they will want their product to be associated.

The advertising manager has personal dealings with key clients and agencies, decides on the appropriate placing of advertisements and supervises their production. He or she organizes special drives and promotions to attract advertising, and is responsible for what can be a considerable number of staff. Most important among these are the salespeople, who are constantly in contact with advertisers and agencies in order to keep abreast of their marketing plans and strategies and to see how their magazine can best fit in with these. On magazines that specialize in 'classified advertisements' the manager is also responsible for large teams of telesales staff, who take down over the phone details of advertisements to be placed and, increasingly, actively sell advertising space, sometimes quite aggressively.

Magazines need advertisers, and it is the advertising manager's job to attract and keep them.

THE EDITORIAL TEAM

Newspapers vary enormously in structure according to whether they are local or national, daily or weekly, broadsheet or tabloid. Nevertheless we can safely generalize that those responsible for producing a newspaper work in three main departments: editorial, production and advertising.

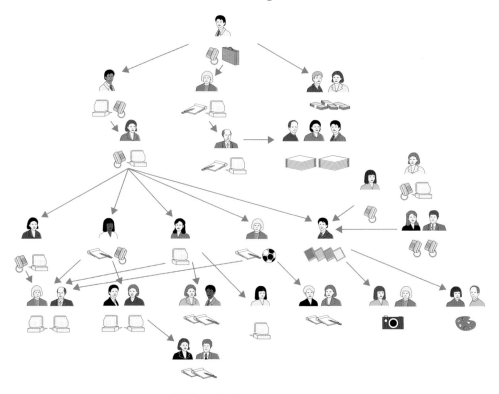

A diagram showing how a typical newspaper staff is structured, with the managing director in charge.

Editorial

This department produces all the stories and features to be found in the paper. On a large national or regional paper the editorial department is divided into separate sections dealing with news, features and sport, and these sections are themselves divided into smaller units. On a small local weekly, however, such specialization may well be an unaffordable luxury, and journalists have to be Jacks (and Jills) of all trades.

It is an often overlooked fact that the staff of a newspaper consists not only of those who find and write the material but also of those who project and process it. The more visible, and some would say more glamorous, side of newspapers consists of reporters and feature writers, but equally important are those involved in every aspect of editing and presentation, such as sub-editors and designers.

> '...bringing out newspapers is a team business rather than an individual business. Though I do think it's important for every newspaper to have some sort of individual stamp to it or else it doesn't have a personality'.
> *The editor of the* Liverpool Echo, *UK*

JOB PROFILE

The Editor

All newspapers have an editor, although what the editor actually does varies widely from one paper to another. Some are writing editors, who tend to write their own leader columns and revise others' stories. Others are more interested in the production process, and focus their attention on presentational matters such as pictures, headlines, layout and the overall visual image of the paper.

Many editors combine the role of journalist with that of manager, writing copy one minute and overseeing the work of other editorial staff the next. Another kind of editor is the political figure, who usually sits on the paper's board of directors and is very publicly identified with the paper's political and social stance. Some editors are a mixture of all the above.

Given the nature of newspapers, there is no such thing as a typical day in the life of an editor. However, the editor usually runs the morning news conference, in order to give editorial direction and shape to the paper. He or she may write one or more of the editorials or 'leaders' and will almost certainly be involved in deciding on the contents and look of the front page. Editors in Britain who have clearly put their stamp on the papers they've edited include Andrew Neil at the *Sunday Times*, Sir David English at the *Mail* and Kelvin Mackenzie at the *Sun*.

Today, many editors have to be managers as well as journalists.

The deputy editor

When the editor is away, the deputy editor takes charge of running the paper. When the editor is present, the deputy usually takes charge of the administration of the office; other than that, their tasks depend very much on what role the editor chooses to play. Next in seniority, on national dailies and on some provincial morning papers, comes the night editor, who is in charge of the paper's production once the main decisions about editorial content have been taken. On a daily paper, their job begins at around 4 pm, on an evening paper as early as 10 am, and consists of deciding which are the most important stories and where they should be placed.

The night editor heads a production team, which may include a deputy and a couple of assistants, as well as the chief sub-editor and the picture editor. The latter's job is to commission graphics and organize the editing of pictures, while sub-editors are responsible for checking facts, correcting errors in spelling and grammar, writing headlines and picture captions, and generally fitting each article into the space available.

A senior sub-editor also performs the vital role of copy-taster, reading every story that is submitted from the in-house newsroom or from news agencies (organizations that gather news and sell it to the various media), and selecting those few which are actually going to be used.

The editor or the deputy editor needs to keep in regular touch with other members of the editorial team.

Section editors

There are also section or department editors such as features editor, news editor and sports editor. These are senior journalists who initiate ideas, co-ordinate departmental activities, decide which stories should be covered and how, brief and organize reporters, set deadlines and cast an experienced editorial eye over the copy. Within the news department, different section editors are responsible for home, foreign and City stories. Meanwhile, within features there are section editors for areas such as the arts, women, television and entertainment, fashion and motoring.

JOB PROFILE

The Features Editor

The features section of the newspaper is the responsibility of the features editor, who works closely with, and answers to, the editor. The features editor attends a daily editorial conference to discuss the stories that are to be covered in the next issue of the paper. This gives the features editor the opportunity to discuss his or her ideas with the editor and other section heads. In particular he or she may want to describe to the pictures editor the type of photographic coverage that is required, and to talk to the news editor about the day's leading stories in case these provide the basis for any particular feature articles.

Once the agenda for the next edition has been decided upon, the features editor meets with the various section editors (arts, media, motoring, fashion and so on) to discuss possible feature ideas. Some of these may well be quite long-term, since the features editor is not always under as much pressure from tight deadlines as, say, the news editor. The features editor also briefs staff writers, commissions pieces from freelancers, checks the finished product, and oversees the department's financial resources. He or she also takes an active writing role on the pages for which they are responsible.

The features editor keeps in constant contact with the section editors to discuss the content of their features.

Editing a magazine

Magazines are organized rather differently to newspapers, for a number of reasons. Firstly, one publisher may well produce a large number of magazines, and these may share the same advertising and production staff. Secondly, magazines tend to have fewer editorial staff, since they commission many articles and features from journalists who are not on the permanent staff and are known as freelancers.

Most magazines are published either weekly or monthly, although there are fortnightlies and quarterlies (magazines that are published four times a year) as well. Working to less tight deadlines than a daily paper, and covering fewer topics, they can employ a smaller core staff. Some monthlies, for instance, may employ only two full-time journalists to oversee publication of the title, whereas a major current affairs weekly such as *Newsweek*, *Time*, the *New Statesman* and *Spectator* will have the full complement of editor, section editors, sub-editors, feature writers, news reporters and designers. Members of staff on smaller magazines may well find their jobs more varied and less narrowly defined than on a bigger one.

This diagram shows how the workforce of a magazine is organized.

The major editorial roles on a magazine are not substantially different from those on a newspaper, although, on consumer and women's titles, editors attempt to establish a rather closer, friendlier relationship with their readers via their leading articles. Magazine editors are also able to plan future issues further ahead than their newspaper counterparts, who are restricted by the immediate daily news agenda.

Magazine journalists can be divided into feature writers and news reporters. However, while on some of the larger magazines these distinctions are fairly rigid, on others news reporters are also expected to produce regular features. This is because, especially in business magazines, features are often more like extended, in-depth news articles. Because of the crucial importance of the look of magazines, feature writers are encouraged to think in terms of the visual presentation of their work and to suggest ideas for suitable pictures and graphics. And, because magazines have more time than newspapers to produce the finished publication, they also have more scope for using images creatively.

The Fashion Editor

Especially in the realm of women's magazines, many titles are sold on their fashion content and reputation alone. This is a highly competitive market, with numerous casualties, and for this reason the job of the fashion editor is an extremely important one. Unlike the fashion editor of a newspaper, the fashion editor of a magazine does not necessarily write any articles. This is because the fashion sections of magazines, whose glossy pages are well suited to the reproduction of glamorous, high-quality photographic images, tend to be far more reliant on pictures than those of newspapers. Consequently, the only writing required is quite often just the production of headlines and captions by the sub-editors.

Fashion editors tend to get their jobs because of their detailed knowledge of fashion and their excellent contacts in the fashion world (which may enable them to run sneak previews of a designer's latest line, for example). The fashion editor is also valued for his or her ability to come up with good ideas for fashion spreads, many of which are planned up to six months in advance of publication.

A first-rate fashion editor is crucial to the success of 'style' magazines.

ORGANIZING THE COVERAGE

However natural a part of our daily lives it may seem, the news doesn't simply write itself on to the page. Of all the billions of events taking place in the world every second of the day, only a very few actually qualify as news. Gathering and spreading the news is a constant process of selection, rejection and refinement.

Planning the content

At the start of each working day on a national paper, the various section editors' first job is to read through the other newspapers, press releases (news items that are typed up and circulated to the press) and news agency reports. They use their editorial judgement to assess the importance

The newsroom is the hub of the news-gathering and news-distribution process.

of these, the progress of stories running on from the previous day(s), and possible stories suggested by reporters. They then draw up the news-list – that is, the issues and events to be included in the next edition of the paper, and the names of the reporters and photographers who will cover them. Many of the items on this list will be diary events, such as press conferences and court proceedings, which can be planned for in advance. These may make the journalist's life easier, but it is the unexpected event which makes it far more interesting and the paper that much more saleable.

Editorial staff attend regular news conferences to decide on which stories will be covered, and with what prominence, by their paper.

The news conference

On a national daily, the news conference usually takes place mid-morning, and may be followed by anything up to six more conferences on a busy news day. A local evening paper usually has its first conference at 9 am; it then holds up to three more during the day. In the case of a local weekly, the conference is held once a week, with updates where necessary. The meeting is attended by the editor and the senior staff (although on a small local paper all staff will probably attend), and the items under discussion are the stories to be included, and where, and with what prominence, they will be positioned in the paper. About three-quarters of what is decided upon at the conference will go into the paper, but allowance must be made for stories developing late in the day, as well as new ones suddenly appearing. This is where the night editor will be expected to exercise his or her judgement.

Gathering the news

The hub of any newspaper is the newsroom which, on a national paper, is staffed up to twenty hours a day. The focus of the newsroom is a series of news desks, each responsible for a different area of the paper's coverage, although a small local paper may have only one such desk. The news desk is where the news coverage of the day is commissioned and co-ordinated.

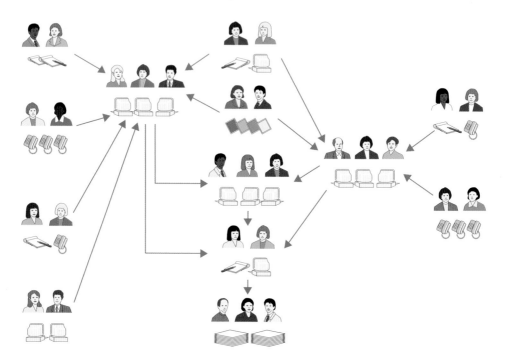

The diagram shows the directions in which news stories travel through the various departments of a newspaper office.

At each desk sits the news editor (on a local paper sometimes the chief reporter), their deputy, and anything up to three reporters. The newsroom also houses a library of useful reference books and recent newspaper files (although, increasingly, material from back issues is called up on the computer screen). As edition times approach, the newsroom is a scene of frantic activity, but it is rarely a quiet place; as one edition of the paper has gone to press, it's time to start working on the next one.

In the process of news-gathering, the most important people are a newspaper's staff reporters. Those magazines that are not entirely features-oriented – for example, weekly current affairs magazines – also employ staff reporters. Other sources of news include agencies, which provide a continuous stream of national, local and international news, and freelance writers of one kind or another. These include local 'stringers', who are frequently journalists on the staff of provincial papers. Stringers sell local stories on a one-off basis to the nationals, either as a means of making extra money or of trying to get a job on a national paper, or both.

Using staff reporters, however, gives a newspaper or magazine the highest degree of control over its news-gathering operation. It also makes it more likely that the paper or magazine will get the all-important 'exclusive' – the key story that no other rival publication has got, and something which is highly sought after in a business as competitive and cut-throat as this.

The staff reporter, and especially one with an excellent list of contacts, is a key player in the news operation.

A national newspaper might have between thirty and sixty reporters in its head office and other news-gathering centres; a local evening paper would have about a quarter of those figures. In some towns and cities, local papers share arrangements for covering court cases and council matters.

Reporters fall into two categories: the specialist and the general. Specialist reporters are also sometimes known as correspondents, and include reporters who specialize in parliamentary business, foreign affairs, the

JOB PROFILE

The News Editor

The job of the news editor is to organize the news-gathering and news-writing activities of the day. This includes planning the coverage of the day's events, assessing the news-worthiness of all information as it comes in from various sources, briefing reporters and local correspondents, and checking news items before they are passed on to the sub-editors.

From the news diary, the news editor prepares a daily schedule showing the stories that are being covered and by whom. A great deal of the rest of the day is spent assessing the value of the information being sent in by reporters and correspondents, reading the endless news agency copy, and discussing the development of stories with reporters ringing in from various locations. The sharpness and thoroughness of a paper's news coverage is ultimately the responsibility of the news editor, and as publication time approaches his or her contribution to the flow of copy is a crucial one. Given the length of the news day, the duties of

the news editor and his or her staff are divided into shifts, which overlap so that maximum coverage is available in the main part of the day.

Preparing the news schedule is one of the first and most important tasks of the news editor's day.

courts, the entertainment world, financial dealings, the media and so on. There are also specifically local correspondents, journalists working on local papers who are accredited by the nationals and the news agencies to cover stories in their area if no staff reporter is available. Such correspondents are usually paid an annual fee in return for which they make their services available as and when they're needed. They are also paid what's called 'lineage' – a payment calculated on the basis of the number of lines of story actually published.

The home news of one country's newspapers is the foreign news of another's, where it will be the responsibility of the foreign news editor. Here the foreign news editor of the Arabic newspaper Al Thawra *discusses the latest stories with the editor.*

GETTING THE STORY

The raw material for newspaper stories comes from a number of sources, of which the most important are news agencies, press releases, press conferences and, of course, journalists themselves.

The flow of information

News agencies collect and supply news, features and pictures to newspapers (and to other organizations such as broadcasters), usually on an annual contract basis. The four biggest international news agencies are Reuters, United Press International, Associated Press and Agence France Press. In Britain the main news agency supplying national news is the Press Association, which is owned by the main provincial newspaper companies. There is also a large number of local and specialist agencies across the country.

News agencies perform a vital function for newspapers. Agencies supply news of events that the newspapers don't have enough staff available to cover directly. They are especially useful for regional newspapers when it comes to national and international events to which they cannot afford to send a reporter. However, as the number of foreign correspondents employed even by major Western dailies has declined in recent years, those papers have become increasingly dependent on the news agencies for foreign news of all kinds. This has led to the criticism by some commentators that newspapers are not reporting foreign news with the thoroughness it deserves, and that the biggest news agencies are monopolizing the flow of news from abroad.

Press conferences and releases

Much of the raw material of the news is actually handed to journalists on a plate. Important events are always heralded by press conferences at which journalists not only get the chance to ask questions but are also supplied with press releases and other forms of newspaper-friendly written material. Meanwhile a torrent of reports of one kind or another, as well as of press releases, flows directly into newspaper offices from company press officers, public relations people, government departments and so on. However, the writers of such reports know that most journalists haven't got time to read them in their entirety and thus include a helpful summary! This deluge of written material flowing constantly into the newspaper office is sometimes known as the 'information subsidy', and it raises some important issues.

Press conferences are a routine source of news stories for journalists.

Watergate

The truly determined and tireless investigative journalist may occasionally be rewarded with a 'scoop'. During the 1972 US presidential election campaign, *Washington Post* journalists Carl Bernstein and Bob Woodward uncovered a groundbreaking story. They revealed that members of staff working for Republican President Richard Nixon had burgled and attempted to bug the headquarters of the Democrats' national committee in the Watergate complex in Washington DC. This became known as the 'Watergate Scandal', and led eventually to Nixon's resignation.

Clearly, it's very useful for the hard-pressed journalist, who is always up against extremely tight deadlines, to be provided free with such large amounts of helpful material. On the other hand, those who provide such information quite clearly, and not unnaturally, have an interest in putting a particular 'spin' on their story. In other words, they present it in a certain light or from a specific angle. This is especially true in an age that has seen a truly massive growth of public relations activities of all kinds and, in particular, the rise of the 'spin doctor'. Never has it been easier, some would argue, for journalists to become mere recyclers of second-hand, and sometimes decidedly tainted, information. Therefore it has never been more important that journalists should approach their work with a critical and sceptical eye.

Doing the calls

At the level of the local press, a daily job which often falls to a young reporter is to check the most commonly used local sources – the police, the hospitals, the local council(s) – to see if any interesting stories have broken. This is generally known as 'doing the calls'. If anything major has happened, the reporter tells his or her news desk, which decides if a journalist needs to cover the story. Similarly, local reporters make it their business to cultivate potentially useful informal contacts with prominent local figures, such as church leaders, head teachers, councillors and business figures.

The General Reporter

As the title implies, the general reporter can be assigned by the news editor or chief reporter to cover any sort of story, either singly or as part of a team. At the heart of journalism lies the source, and becoming a good journalist is, to a large extent, a matter of developing sources.

A reporter needs to be prepared to work long hours, to visit unlikely places at awkward moments, and meet a wide range of people, often in difficult circumstances. Above all, the reporter needs to know where to go in order to find the information they need. Some facts can be ascertained and checked in reference books, archives, newspaper cuttings files, via a telephone enquiry or over the internet. However, the reporter also needs an excellent range of personal contacts, and the most treasured possession of any journalist is the book or computer file in which their sources' contact details are listed.

If detailed information on a particular topic has already reached the newspaper, the reporter is briefed accordingly. However, sometimes the information on which the assignment is based is wrong and the story 'falls down'. Therefore, when the reporter comes to file the story, he or she must have checked the facts, talked to the people concerned and put together the account in a readable form.

The general reporter needs to cultivate a wide range of reliable sources of news stories.

Developing good interviewing skills is a vital part of the reporter's job. Above, the former Russian leader, Mikhail Gorbachev (right) is interviewed by a US political commentator.

Interview skills

Knowing the right people to talk to is a vital part of the journalist's job, but it's equally important to know how to interview them. This can be done in either a formal or informal way, the latter often being more appropriate if the interviewee is not a public figure and therefore not used to being interviewed. All interviews need to be recorded, either in writing (in which case it's desirable to know shorthand) or on tape. If the interviewee has agreed to speak only 'off the record', then nothing they say may be directly attributed to them in print. However, such interviews can be very useful to the journalist in providing background information, and direct quotes can still be used if they are attributed to 'a source close to the story' or to some other similarly vague and anonymous figure.

Interviewing may look easy enough on the surface, but it is a fine art and one that is extremely hard to master. Time may be short, the surroundings not conducive to conversation (this applies particularly to telephone interviews or those conducted in noisy and crowded public places), the interviewee nervous, intimidating or untrustworthy, and so on. It is therefore crucial that the reporter has a well-prepared list of relevant questions, and doesn't waste time skating around the topic or asking questions to which a little elementary research would easily provide the answers. It's also important to find out as much as possible about the interviewee before talking to them.

Media Fact

The Hitler diaries

Every journalist wants a scoop. However, sometimes this desire can lead to a newspaper being hoaxed. In 1983 Rupert Murdoch's News Corporation paid $400,000 for the right to publish in the *Sunday Times* what it claimed to be Hitler's diaries. These turned out to be a crude forgery.

The copy

Once the journalist has all the necessary facts in their possession, they have to write the story, or what is known in the newspaper business as the 'copy'. This frequently used to be taken down over the telephone by copytakers, but is now increasingly transmitted to the office in electronic form. Alternatively the journalist may return to his or her desk to write the story. Delivering the finished story is known as 'filing the copy'.

When writing any story, a reporter must above all remember that the main questions needing an answer are: who, what, when, where, why and how? Stories need to be written in a style that is factual and concise, as space is limited, and to open with a paragraph, or 'intro', that contains the essential points of the story and will attract and hold the reader's attention.

Once the reporter has gathered all the elements of the story, she needs to put them together in a way that is easy to understand and will attract and hold the reader's interest.

Of course, many news events carry on developing long after the reporter has filed his or her copy, and such stories have to be updated in subsequent editions of that day's or evening's paper, as well as over the following days if necessary. Such stories are known as 'running' stories.

PUTTING THE STORY ON THE PAGE

As we have seen, the journalistic staff of any newspaper or magazine can be divided into those who find and write the material, be it features or news stories, and those who edit it. So, within a newspaper or magazine office, we can make a useful distinction between gatherers and processors. The latter include the journalists who are responsible for making sure not only that articles are accurate, well written and conform to the house style, but also look good on the page and encourage readers actually to read them.

In such intensely competitive businesses as the national newspaper and magazine industries, the 'look' of a publication, the way in which it actually presents itself, is an extremely important marketing factor. This helps to explain why, on both newspapers and magazines, reporters, feature writers and photographers tend to be outnumbered by editorial staff of one kind or another.

The picture editor plays a key role in making stories attractive and readable.

Technological change

During the last twenty years, the production of newspapers and magazines has undergone a technological revolution. This has transformed not only the product but also the working lives of hundreds of thousands of people employed in the industry. Whereas once upon a time, articles were made up of strips of printed paper which had to be stuck on to the page layout with glue, everything now arrives, is processed and despatched in electronic form via computer. Similarly, databases, dictionaries and cuttings files can increasingly be called up online and consulted on screen.

Pasting-up typeset copy by hand, below, is a thing of the past. In modern newspapers and magazines this task is done using a computer.

The main production job on any daily paper concerns the news and sports pages. As edition times approach, it is here that the sub-editors assemble the pages under the control of the chief sub-editor and the 'back bench' (usually the night editor, their deputy, and one or two assistants). In the case of the sports pages, it's the sports editor who is in charge. The news and sports pages make up the bulk of a daily paper's content and are the ones at which the majority of incoming copy is directed. The sub-editing of the features pages is carried out separately and under less pressure of time, since much of the material will have been planned and delivered well in advance of the material for the news pages.

A national daily employs at least twenty sub-editors, or subs as they are universally known, whereas a local evening paper has about a dozen. Larger dailies traditionally had a subs desk divided into top-table and down-table sections, although the introduction of computer technology has rather blurred this distinction.

Media Fact

A new era

In the early 1960s, computers first began to make their way into the newspaper production process. Two of the key pioneers in the United States were the *Los Angeles Times* and *Oklahoma City Times*. In Canada, the first instances of computerization in the newspaper industry took place at the Toronto-based *Globe* and *Mail*, the *Daily Star* and the *Telegram*.

Today, photographers can send digital images instantly to the news desk by electronic means.

The Sub-Editor

Top-table subs, or their modern equivalents, are usually senior, experienced journalists who can quickly assess the importance of a story and know where best to position it for maximum impact. They are responsible for designing the actual page layouts or 'shapes', which arrive at their desk with clearly marked spaces indicating where the advertising department has sold space. They will also have a set of stories from the news desk.

From the daily news conference the sub is likely to know what story is to be the main focal point of the page, and will mark out its position on the page, indicating where pictures or graphics should go, the size of the headline and so on. This process will continue with all the other stories on the page, taking particular care to achieve maximum coherence and readability, as well as adhering to the all-important overall 'look' of the paper, which means using only certain specific typefaces, sizes of headline and so on.

The top-table subs also instruct the down-table ones, who deal more with the copy itself than the construction of pages as whole. The job of the down-table subs includes the following:

- checking the facts of a story;
- checking grammar, spelling and readability;
- ensuring that the house style has been adhered to;
- rewriting poorly written stories, or putting together a story from several different sources;
- editing the text to fit exactly into its allotted space (this is known as 'casting off');
- ensuring that the story is legally safe, consulting the paper's legal staff if required;
- giving the computer the appropriate commands so that the story is set in the right type and measure for its allotted place on the page;
- revising the story for later editions, or in the light of editorial decisions taken at a higher level (this is called a 'rejig', 'redress' or 'dress');
- providing captions for pictures or graphics;
- writing headlines (although for the main stories the headlines may have already been decided upon as part of the page strategy).

The sub-editor is an important 'processor' of stories written by others, ensuring that they are readable and well-placed.

In some ways, the arrival of computer technology has changed the subs' work considerably, in others less so. The sub still needs traditional editing skills – although the computer can make the process of editing easier and quicker, it cannot instill those skills into a journalist who lacks them!

Making up the pages

However, the coming of the computer has meant the complete disappearance of what used to be called the composing room. This was where printing staff physically arranged the type – made up of individual letters on small blocks of metal – in lines and columns.

A vanished era: a composing room in China in the old 'hot metal' days.

The advent of new technology has thrust the responsibility for making up and preparing pages for press on to the subs themselves. As we have seen, pages are now built up wholly on screen within the editorial department itself. Even pictures and graphics, after cropping and scaling by the art desk, are imaged into the page by means of scanners, while advertisements are input electronically from the advertising production department.

Such changes were brought about at the expense of considerable job losses in the newspaper production sector. The job losses were fewer in the magazine sector, in which new technology, at least in Britain, was introduced in a more gradual and rather less brutal way.

The introduction of new ways of producing and distributing newspapers frequently met with resistance from the workforce, as here in New York during the 1970s.

News International

On 23 January 1986, newspaper proprietor Rupert Murdoch moved the production of his four British papers into a new, computerized plant in London's Docklands. Breaking with past tradition in the UK, Murdoch's new operation, News International, did not recognize the existing trade unions or the rights of their members. More than 5,000 print workers and clerical staff were sacked at a stroke. Rupert Murdoch's strong-arm, union-busting tactics made the introduction of new production technology to his newspaper titles in the UK and the US a particularly fraught affair.

On the one hand, we now have cleaner, better-produced and more-stylish looking newspapers, and some journalists enjoy the degree of input which editorial staff now have into the finished product. On the other hand, others feel that they are being forced to carry out more and more tasks and generally to work harder and harder in an increasingly insecure and competitive environment. Journalism is generally recognized as being a highly stressful job, and one whose practitioners are particularly prone to the repetitive strain injury (RSI) which afflicts heavy users of keyboards.

THE IMPORTANCE OF DESIGN

Newspapers, whether national or local, are published in two main sizes: tabloid and broadsheet. Tabloids are easier to use and appeal to those who have either little time or inclination to read a great deal. The tabloid size lends itself to the bold, dramatic, easy-to-read layout pioneered, in the United Kingdom, by the *Daily Mirror*, and in the United States by various newspapers in the aftermath of the First World War. The larger pages of the broadsheets are better suited to longer news stories and feature articles.

The newspaper is a very carefully designed product: there is nothing haphazard about the way in which items appear daily on its pages. There's a deliberate balance maintained between news and features, and between both of these and the advertising copy. Words must relate to images, and vice-versa, and both of these elements must work together in the context both of the individual page and of the paper as a whole.

Pictures on a page

Design is vital in highlighting various items and in indicating their relative importance. On each page, headlines, text and pictures are used to form an eye-catching shape to attract attention. As the reader turns the pages, the various sizes and weights of type indicate the relative importance of each story, while special type motifs highlight regular features.

Media Fact

Today

Britain's first full-colour daily newspaper, and also its first produced with computerized technology, was *Today*, which was launched in 1986. In financial terms it was never a success, and finally closed in 1995. However, its innovations in production and design were soon copied by other more successful papers.

Design is largely a matter of placing elements in relation to one another, and page design aims to position words and images in such a way that the eye is encouraged to move easily around the page and look at the various items on it. The main headline and the lead picture are obviously the focal points of the page, and other bold visual items, such as advertisements, have to be positioned so as not to detract or distract from them. Large bodies of text are made easier on the eye by being broken up by sub-headings and by making use of variations in type sizes.

Newspaper pages need to attract the reader in the first place, and then hold their attention. Good design plays a crucial role in both these processes.

headline
lead picture
motif
folio
cartoon
sub-heading
advert
caption

Today, when the look of a magazine or newspaper is a key selling point, the job of the designer is extremely important.

Familiarity and ease of use are key ingredients in newspaper design. Everything has its usual appointed place, so that the reader knows where to look for the articles that are of most interest to him or her: the main stories on the front page, sport at the back, the editorial and comment pages near the middle, and so on. Similarly, certain kinds of article are always presented in the same way, with particular typefaces and in their own distinctive layout. However, as long as certain basic elements of presentation and design are adhered to, there is still room for considerable variation in the look of individual pages.

The importance of design as a crucial part of any product's appeal was recognized as far back as the first half of the nineteenth century. In the latter part of the twentieth century it became something of an obsession, as 'designer labels' were no longer exclusive to the world of high fashion but were worn by style-conscious members of the general public. The printed word was also affected by these developments.

Defining the brand

Newspapers are designed in such a way as to distinguish one from another by their different visual characters, but also, even more importantly, to attract and hold the reader's eye. It's a process very similar to the packaging of other products, for example, different brands of soap powder. Most newspapers, whether tabloid or broadsheet, have created their own separate design departments or art desks, where the pages are drawn in detail, the typefaces chosen and the pictures edited under the supervision of an art editor or art director. Such is the importance of design to the contemporary newspaper's identity, that periodic redesigns become news items in their own right! Significantly, the *Guardian* headline over a story about its 1999 redesign was: 'Design to create pages people want to read'.

In our image-conscious society, many newspapers feel the need to go in for regular redesigns.

Design plays an especially important role in the fiercely competitive world of magazine publishing.

netnames NEWS n³

issue 11_2000

Battling the Domain Drain

PROFILED: TIM BERNERS-LEE – FATHER OF THE WEB
FEATURE: PROTECTING YOUR TRADEMARK ONLINE
PLUS ICANN'S PROGRESS AND THE YOKOHAMA SUMMIT, THE NEW DOMAIN NAME DISPUTES PROCEDURE, NIC NEWS, DOMAIN STATS AND MUCH MORE INSIDE...

net names
NetBenefit Group

Media Fact

The design revolution

Between 1981 and 1986, Neville Brody's design work at the *Face* magazine revolutionized magazine design, deliberately abandoning what had become the taken-for-granted conventions of 'good' layout and typography. Brody mixed typefaces and invented new ones, stretched photographs and blurred and intermingled them with the text. Design became a highly visible aspect of the magazine rather than a neutral envelope in which to deliver the text as unobtrusively as possible.

Design is equally, if not more, important in the field of magazine publishing. Here vast numbers of titles jostle for the reader's attention, and titles aimed at similar readerships desperately vie to make themselves more attractive than their rivals. Long before the potential consumer has read a word, the look of a magazine has begun to communicate a great deal about it – not just what it's about, but who it's aimed at, its values and aspirations, and so on. The cover, which can be considered as the magazine's 'face', plays a particularly vital role here. As one graphic designer put it: 'It has to sell the general concept of the publication as well as to reflect, through its design, the intellectual level of the editorial content.' Furthermore, it has to do this extremely rapidly and in the crowded environment of the newsagent, crowded not only with milling shoppers but also with numerous competing titles.

The Picture Editor

For many magazine readers, the images are one of the key reasons for buying a particular publication. These can either be photographs or artwork (drawing, computer graphic, photomontage, cartoon and so on). On a large, consumer-type magazine, the decision about what kind of illustrations to use in a particular article will be taken by the picture editor. If, for example, the picture editor has been offered a particularly interesting portfolio of images and is looking for a piece of writing to accompany them, the pictures may even sometimes precede the article.

Picture editing is, essentially, the process whereby photographs and other illustrations are created, selected and assembled from a variety of sources. A great deal of the picture editor's skill lies in knowing how and where to get hold of the desired images as quickly and cheaply as possible, although bigger publications may employ picture researchers to do this job. If images are to be commissioned, however, a picture editor, often working with the art director, has to decide whether to use a photographer or another kind of illustrator. He or she also has to select the right person for the job and then brief them fully, as well as set budgets and deadlines. Here the picture editor also needs a wide range of contacts and a good knowledge of the contemporary visual art scene.

The picture editor also has to know just which images to use from the potentially vast array on offer. This may sound easy, but it actually takes a great deal of skill and experience to spot the right picture, to know if it needs cropping or colour correcting (and if so, how) and then be able to set it off to best advantage in an imaginative layout.

The picture editor needs to know where to find the right images, and how to select the most appropriate ones.

THE PRODUCTION PROCESS

Many early newspapers were founded, owned and run by printers, and today most national newspaper and many magazine proprietors own the plants at which their publications are printed. Nearly all of these facilities print more than one newspaper or magazine, either because they are owned jointly by a consortium of different proprietors, or because the proprietor owns a number of different publications.

The printing of numerous papers and magazines at centralized sites, many of which may well be at a considerable geographical distance from their editorial offices, has been made possible by the recent developments in information technology. In particular, the ability to transmit fully made-up pages in electronic form means that printing plates (the thin, metal sheet from which the page is actually printed) can be made at the printing plant. As a consequence, printing plants can be built outside large urban centres, thus reducing the costs of both labour and land. They can also be arranged around the country in such a way as to shorten delivery times to newspaper and magazine wholesalers. This saves on transport costs and, in many countries,

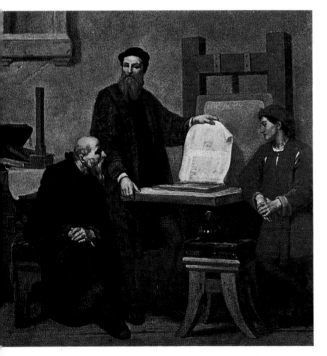

Johannes Gutenberg is generally regarded as having invented printing in fifteenth-century Germany.

ensures that even geographically remote areas can receive relatively late editions of newspapers. Furthermore, printing several publications in one plant considerably cuts down production costs.

Hot metal

Until the second half of the twentieth century, newspapers and magazines were produced with a technology dating back to Johannes Gutenberg in the first half of the fifteenth century and perfected in the nineteenth. To summarize a lengthy and complex process, the text of articles was set from the journalist's edited copy, which contained all the appropriate instructions from the sub-editors, on to linotype machines. As the operator entered the text into the machine by means of a keyboard, it formed lines of type of the right length. The operator then injected molten metal so as to take an impression of each line. As the lines cooled they could be set in sequence on a metal tray or 'galley', and in this way the individual lines were built up into articles and the articles arranged into pages. This process was known as 'composing'.

After each article was set, an inked proof was taken, so that proof readers could check the text for errors. The pages of type, along with metal blocks of images, were arranged according to instructions from the editorial department and held together by metal frames. These completed pages were known as 'formes', and they provided the basis for a mould from which, again using molten metal, a plate was made from which the page could be printed in the machine room.

Days gone by: an operator entering text into a linotype machine.

Media Fact

Linotype

Between 1815 and 1871, around seventy attempts were made to create and patent a machine which could quickly set type and adjust the spaces of words. It was not until 1892 that what was effectively the first linotype machine went on sale. The machine was the work of a German, Ottmar Mergenthaler, who had emigrated to the United States in 1872.

New technology

Checking pages at their photographic stage.

The new electronic technology came first to newspapers and magazines in the United States in the 1960s, and then elsewhere. But poor industrial relations, composed equally of management incompetence and union inflexibility, delayed its introduction to the British national press until the mid-1980s. What this technology did was quite simply to wipe out the need for traditional typesetting, in other words all of the technology that went into the making of the printing plate described earlier.

Using a light box for closer inspection.

Making a photographic plate.

Not only could journalists input their copy directly, but plates could also be made much more quickly and effectively, thanks to the development of photo-composition. Pages are now composed photographically, and the negative image burned by bright light into the thin, photosensitive plates used in the printing process. Especially when accompanied by improvements in printing technology, it made for cleaner and clearer print and better picture reproduction, and paved the way for colour printing. The main drawback was the high cost of buying new equipment, but expenditure here could ultimately be offset against the sale of old printing plants and large-scale redundancies.

Electronic transmission

A key development in newspaper and magazine production has been the growth of various forms of electronic transmission. The earliest of these was the facsimile, but given recent developments in computer technology, it is now possible to send fully made-up pages from the main editorial offices at the click of a mouse. These are then received at the main production

Media Fact

The invention of the facsimile

By the late 1840s, at least two prototype facsimile systems had been developed in the United States – the 'chemical telegraph' and the 'copying telegraph'. However, it was not until the early 1970s that the modern facsimile machine began to be developed. By the end of 1985, Japan had 850,000 fax installations, the United States 550,000 and Europe 120,000.

centres, unscrambled, re-formed and turned into printing plates.

It was once thought that the facsimile method would be a good way of sending a newspaper to its readers, and this was first tried, using radio signals, by the *St Louis Post-Dispatch* in the United States in 1938. After the Second World War, the *Asahi Shimbun* newspaper repeated the experiment in Japan, but it proved too expensive to be a viable commercial proposition. However, it was the Japanese in the 1960s who first established the regular use of facsimile transmission for multi-centre newspaper production.

A futuristic looking newspaper office.

In this way, a totally new, electronic system of producing newspapers was developed, with, at one end of the process, the text being directly input by journalists, and, at the other, after editing, planning and page design, emerging as a printing plate. Along the way, a large number of jobs have been lost in the production centres, and journalists have had to learn a whole range of new skills and take on new responsibilities.

After the revolution

Newspapers today are bigger, cleaner, more colourful and better styled. However, in Britain at least, the much-heralded technological revolution has signally failed to live up to one of its main promises, namely that it would increase the number and variety of national daily papers by lowering production costs and making it easier for new players to enter the marketplace. Nor has the press fared much better in many other European countries which have seen newspaper closures as a result of declining readerships and advertising revenue. In Britain, the first national paper to introduce the complete new technology package, Eddie Shah's *Today*, soon found itself absorbed into Rupert Murdoch's global media empire, never made a profit and finally closed in 1995.

Hot off the press: checking and colour-correcting the printed page.

When the production process is complete, the printed newspapers are distributed to newsagents around the country.

The fact of the matter is that setting up and running a newspaper is a very expensive business – and the cost factor is something that the new technology has done nothing to change. And, in a highly competitive marketplace, established players will do their utmost to make life as difficult as possible for the new entrant. It is probably in the magazine sector that the new technology has had the most beneficial effects, making possible radical improvements to those all-important aspects of illustration and design. Meanwhile, what is known as 'desktop publishing' has enabled a raft of smaller, specialist publications not only to enter the market but also to survive there and even make a profit.

NEWSPAPERS AND MAGAZINES

The Production Manager

The production manager's task is to oversee the production and printing of (usually) several newspapers and magazines. This involves constantly reading and checking the copy for errors as well as keeping an eagle eye on the quality of the printing itself.

An early stage of the process involves setting the advertisements, scanning in all the pictures (both editorial and advertising), and creating the graphics that are needed. The advertisements are sent electronically to the editorial teams so that they can incorporate them in their page layouts. When the teams have done their work and the pages are complete then the production department, under the supervision of the production manager, makes the aluminium plates for the press. Once the printing press has been plated up, it begins running, and between 500-1,000 copies are printed until the print quality is crisp and clean (or 'in register'). During this period, the press is constantly adjusted to achieve the best quality printing. The early test copies are dumped and, once the press is running to the production manager's satisfaction, it can print between 40,000 and 50,000 copies per hour.

Working in the production department requires a variety of different skills, including illustrative ones. It is important to have computer skills, a fine eye for detail and design, and an ability to meet tight deadlines.

The production manager casts his watchful eye over the printing process.

GETTING A JOB IN THE INDUSTRY

People are attracted to a job in newspaper or magazine journalism for a variety of reasons – because they enjoy writing, or because they think it's glamorous and exciting, or maybe because they believe in the importance of informing people about the world in which they live.

> '...journalism is a skill that can only be acquired on the job and at the end of the day it depends on whether someone has a burning individual talent'.
> *Sir David English, a former editor of the* Daily Mail

Born to the job, or trained?

So, how do you become a journalist? Some would argue that the only way to learn to be a journalist is 'on the job'. Their advice would be to get a job – any job, be it ever so humble – on a local paper or small magazine, and work your way up to the world of national newspapers and magazines. However, there is a school of thought which holds that journalism is a profession with its own codes of practice and standards, and that these can and should be taught and assessed via thorough training, both before entering the profession and in the workplace itself.

Academic qualifications

Good academic qualifications are increasingly a must. Whether or not they are graduates, 40 per cent of all entrants to newspaper journalism in the UK start on a local paper, where they receive training for a period of between eighteen months and two years. At the end of this time they have to pass seven qualifying examinations and then go on to take the NCTJ National Certificate Examination. Another useful entry

point is through the burgeoning magazine sector, and most of the major magazine publishers run in-house training schemes in conjunction with the Periodicals Training Council. In Britain, about 80 per cent of new entrants to this sector are graduates or have had some full-time education beyond A-levels.

Would-be journalists are strongly advised to contribute to their school or college newspaper so that they can turn up to interviews with a bulging cuttings file! They should also seize any other opportunity to have their work published, as well as to build up useful contacts in the industry. Furthermore, with newspapers and magazines increasingly shedding full-time and permanent staff and making more and more use of freelancers, they could also think about following the freelance life. This certainly makes for a varied, if insecure existence, though it lacks the undoubted benefits to be gained from being trained in-house at someone else's expense!

However powerful they may be, great national leaders – in this case Nelson Mandela and Bill Clinton – need to appear regularly before the world's press.

Media Fact

Studying journalism

The world's first journalism school was founded in 1908 at the University of Missouri. By 1940 there were over 500 schools in the United States offering journalism courses. Today around 325 colleges and universities offer programmes in which students can major in journalism.

Academic qualifications

However, it's important to remember that not all jobs on such publications involve journalistic

writing skills. Given the crucial importance today of the look of newspapers and magazines, designers, graphic artists and photographers play a key role in these sectors of the publications industry. And, on the production side, printing, electrical and information technology skills are much needed. A wide range of educational qualifications is useful if you are considering one of the many types of jobs available in newspapers and magazines.

Familiarity with the various aspects of new technology is vital for almost any job in newspapers or magazines.

Behind the headlines

What this book has attempted to show is that there are many more jobs in journalism than the most prominent one of the by-lined reporter or feature writer on a major newspaper. On newspapers there are armies of editorial and production staff working away out of the limelight, and beyond the national daily and Sunday press there are the local and national papers and vast swathes of magazines of one kind or another. The jobs that these provide are many and varied, although all of them tend to be lumped together under the heading of 'journalism', so prospective journalists would be well-advised to think about what kind of job in the profession they actually want to pursue.

They should also try to put behind them the many myths about journalism fostered by the movies – and, of course, by journalists themselves. Not all journalism is exciting and well paid – much of it is routine, badly rewarded and stressful. Few are ever going to become crusading journalists fighting for great humanitarian causes. But many a hapless hack will be ordered to cover a story that they consider intrusive, trivial or simply downright distasteful. In this respect it's worth remembering that journalists actually rank pretty low in the public's estimation.

On the other hand, widely disseminated information is one of the wellsprings of democracy, and newspapers and magazines are among its chief conduits. So, despite the excesses of the late twentieth-century popular press, it is important to recognize the enormous benefits we reap in the way of both information and entertainment from the vast array of newspapers and magazines available to us today.

In modern, democratic societies the world over, newspapers and magazines are an important source of information.

'...the basis of our government being the opinion of the people, the first object should be to keep that right; and were it left to me to decide whether we should have a government without newspapers or newspapers without government, I should not hesitate to prefer the latter.' *The early nineteenth-century US president, Thomas Jefferson*

GLOSSARY

to brief to inform or instruct someone thoroughly before they undertake a particular task

by-line the journalist's name attached to their particular story or feature

caption a short piece of text accompanying and explaining the significance of a photograph or other visual image

circulation the number of copies sold of each issue

copy the material of a newspaper or magazine article before it is actually printed

cropping (of photos) trimming a photograph, either to fit the available space or to isolate a particular detail of the complete picture

deadline the time by which work must be delivered if it is to be published in the appropriate edition of the newspaper or magazine

diary events events that are known about in advance, such as anniversaries of important occurrences and state visits

editorial the space, usually in the middle of a newspaper but at the start of a magazine, in which the publication's own views on particular matters are expressed

filing (a story) when the journalist delivers his or her copy

freelancers journalists who are not on the permanent staff of a newspaper or magazine but who are paid for each piece of copy they produce

graphics illustrations other than photographs

hack a slang term for a journalist or writer

house style the style of writing adopted by a particular magazine or newspaper

news conference a meeting in a newspaper's offices to decide on what stories will be included, where they will be positioned, and with what prominence, in the next edition

niche very specific part of a particular market

photomontage an image assembled from two or more separate photographs

portfolio a collection of the best work assembled by a writer, photographer or designer; particularly useful for impressing potential employers

press conference an event organized by an individual or organization to disseminate a particular item of news to the press

proof a trial impression of an article, used for making corrections and changes before printing

source/sources something, or more usually someone, to whom a journalist turns for the information that they need

stringer a regular newspaper correspondent who is nonetheless not on the permanent staff

trade union an organized association of employees formed to protect and further their rights, particularly regarding pay and working conditions

typeface a set of letters in a specific design

typesetting arranging the type as it is finally going to appear on the printed page

USEFUL ADDRESSES

The following websites cover aspects of the newspaper and magazine industries:

http://www.bpif.org.uk – British Printing Industries Federation, 11 Bedford Row, London WC1R 4DX

http://www.gpmu.org.uk – Graphical, Paper and Media Union, Keys House, 63-67 Bromham Road, Bedford MK40 2AG

http://www.Globalprint.com/uk/iop – Institute of Printing, The Mews, Hill House, Clanricarde Road, Tunbridge Wells, Kent TN1 1PJ

http://www.nuj.org.uk – National Union of Journalists, Headland, 308-312 Gray's Inn Road, London WC1X 8DP

http://www.nctj.com – National Council for the Training of Journalists, Latton Bush Centre, Southern Way, Harlow, Essex CM18 7BL. (The best place to start if you want to find out about training courses in the UK.)

http://www.manchesteronline.co.uk – Newspapers in Education, Manchester Evening News, 164 Deansgate, Manchester M60 2RD

http://www.newspapersoc.org.uk – Newspaper Society, Bloomsbury House, 74-77 Great Russell Street, London WC1B 3DA

http://www.ppa.co.uk – Periodical Publishers Association, Queen's House, 28 Kingsway, London WC2B 6JR

Visit learn.co.uk for more resources.

BOOKS TO READ

Readers may find the following books useful:

Creative Newspaper Design, V Giles and F W Hodgson, Focal Press, 1996

Essential English: for Journalists, Editors and Writers, H Evans, Pimlico, 2000

Inside Journalism, S Niblock, Blueprint, 1996

Magazine Design, C Foges, Roto Vision, 1999

The Magazines Handbook, J McKay, Routledge, 2000

Modern Newspaper Practice, F W Hodgson, Focal Press, 1996

New Magazine Design, W Owen, Calmann, 1991

Newspaper Layout and Design, D Moen, Iowa State University Press, 2000

The Newspapers Handbook, R Keeble, Routledge, 1998

Pictures on a Page, H Evans, Pimlico, 1997

The Universal Journalist, D Randall, Pluto, 2000

INDEX

Numbers in **bold** refer to illustrations.